Coals of Fire
by Unknown

Copyright © 2019 by HardPress

Address:
HardPress
8345 NW 66TH ST #2561
MIAMI FL 33166-2626
USA
Email: info@hardpress.net

COALS OF FIRE

A Tale of Former Days.

TRANSLATED FROM THE GERMAN

"If thine enemy hunger, feed him; if he thirst, give him drink: for in so doing thou shalt heap coals of fire on his head." —Romans xii. 20.

LONDON:
Printed by Truscott, Son, and Simmons,
Suffolk-lane, City.

COALS OF FIRE.

CHAPTER I.

It was a beautiful summer's evening. The red and gold clouds round the setting sun were clearly reflected on the surface of a broad lake, whose waves broke gently on the shore, as the soft breeze ruffled its blue waters; the same breeze stirred the foliage of the surrounding woods, which sloped down almost to the water's edge. But in several places the wood was cleared away, and here and there, in the open spaces, white-washed log-houses were seen, which shone like silver against the dark trees in the background. On a gentle rising ground, near the lake, stood a house somewhat larger than the others, surrounded by a number of smaller huts, which were used as barns, stables, and cow-houses. Further inland other log-huts were visible, and between each were fruitful kitchen-gardens and broad tracts of arable land, in which grew wheat, Indian corn, and many kinds of vegetables.

The whole had the appearance of a flourishing settlement. The owner lived in the large house on the hill, whose windows shone in the evening sun. He was a robust, cheerful old man, more than seventy years of age. He had worked industriously through youth and manhood, and now he was able to rest with a light heart and a good conscience, still superintending those to whom he had entrusted the care of his property.

Marcus Stucker (for that was the old man's name) was sitting before his house. In front of him stretched the beautiful lake, with its background of high mountains covered with trees, which seemed on all sides to encircle the lake like an emerald ring. The hour of rest had just struck, and the tired labourers were gladly returning to their homes. With them came Martin's son Augustine, with his wife and his six children, to spend the evening hours with the old man. Some talk was exchanged between father and son about the day's work, and then the old man played with his young grandchildren, who dearly loved the old man.

"What a glorious evening it is!" exclaimed Julius, the eldest boy; "and what a beautiful country this is," he added. "Grandfather, is there any place in Europe as beautiful as this?"

The old man smiled, and said, as he stroked the boy's fair hair, "Europe is a beautiful land; and Germany, our native country, is a glorious part of Europe."

"What!" exclaimed Julius, in surprise, "is not our America our native place?"

"Yes; it is yours, and your father's, and mine," the old man replied; "but the

Fatherland of your great-grandfather, who has now been dead many a long year, was Germany."

"Then why did our great-grandfather come here?" asked Julius's brother Marcus—a boy of eleven; "if Germany is as beautiful as you say it is, grandfather, why did he leave it?"

"Because God's hand led him here," said the old man, reverently; "and to our ancestor's goodness do we owe our happy home in this land. Your great-grandfather's life was, in many respects, a very remarkable one."

"Oh! tell us all about it, grandfather," the children cried, with one voice; "tell us all about it."

The old man told them he was ready to do what they wished, so the children sat round him in a circle on the ground, and listened attentively to his story.

"It is now more than eighty years ago," he began, since a merchant, named Martin

Stucker, lived in a small inland German town. He was always looked upon as a rich —or, at least, a well-to-do man, who lived a honest and upright life. His family consisted of his wife, one son, and three daughters, who were all brought up by their parents in the fear of God. Augustine, the only son, was always a good and dutiful child. As he grew older, he showed both industry and talent, and his tutor often spoke highly of him to his father, whose wish was his son should succeed him in his business; but, on receiving so many proofs of his unusual abilities, he resolved he should be sent to college instead, and become a learned man.

According to his father's wishes and his own inclinations, he devoted himself to the study of medicine; and with deep delight did his mother look forward to the future, when she hoped to see her dear son settled in his native town as a doctor. This, too, was Augustine's great desire: little did he think, as he studied hard for this end, what a widely different career awaited him.

Augustine was just on the point of ending his college life, when he received news that destroyed all his hopes at one blow. One morning he received a letter from home, sealed with black; he opened it with a trembling hand, and read these words, written by his mother:—"My poor boy, come home at once; your father has lost all he possessed, through the fraud of a false friend, and the shock has killed him. May God help us all in our bitter sorrow!"

Sorrowfully did Augustine gather together his possessions, and hasten to his home. Till now his return had always been greeted with the brightest joy by both parents and sisters, but now he was met with speechless sorrow; his mother and sisters clung around him, their thoughts being full of him who was always the first to welcome home his dear boy. How little had they thought, when father and son last parted, that they were never to meet again on earth!

Augustine asked eagerly for particulars of all that had happened. His mother told him how a false friend, on whose opinion her husband had the most unfortunate reliance, had persuaded him to embark his whole fortune in a doubtful speculation, in which his so-called friend was deeply interested, and to his management the whole was entrusted. This man secretly disappeared one night with all the money that was in his charge, and never was he heard of again by those whom he had so grossly deceived.

Augustine required some little time to recover from these successive crushing blows; but trust in God soon brought back his accustomed hopefulness and cheerfulness. He saw he was now the only stay and support of his widowed mother and young sisters, and carefully did he consider the steps he must take to secure his family from beggary. He examined his father's books and papers with the greatest care, and then endeavoured to collect the scattered remains of his father's possessions.

Alas! it was a very small sum he could thus realise: hardly enough for the family to subsist upon for two years, even with the strictest economy. To finish his studies was quite impossible; and this, which was a cause of great regret to himself, was a still greater sorrow to his mother.

"What will become of you, my dear boy?" she said, with tears, when Augustine had put the whole state of affairs before her: "all your hard study and perseverance will have been thrown away. What do you think of doing?"

Augustine's own heart was sad enough, but he tried to answer his mother cheerfully. "Don't think about me, mother: my education will not have been thrown away; if it is of no use to me now, it will be at some other time. Let us take comfort, and trust to our Father in heaven. He who tempers the wind to the shorn lamb, will take care of us. I can work: I am young, and healthy. God will direct me how to provide for you and my sisters."

Augustine's gentle, tender words soothed his mother's grief, and made her think more hopefully of the future, while he anxiously considered how to provide for his family. He visited his father's friends, and asked their advice, but they gave him little encouragement. Next he tried to obtain a situation as a tutor or teacher, but without success, for he was told he was too young; then he tried to gain something by writing, but the little he earned was too uncertain to be much help.

As he sat one evening at his desk, leaning his weary head upon his hands, he thought sadly enough of the future. The small sum he had saved from the wreck of his father's fortune was fast diminishing, and nowhere could he see any reasonable hope of providing for his family. At length he got up restlessly, and went down-stairs to his father's office, and again looked through his papers to see if he could not find some little debt still owing to him. But his search was vain, and with a sigh he replaced the books. As he was doing so, he noticed in the back of the cupboard a tin box which he did not remember to have seen before. He took it out; the key was in the lock; he opened it, and looked in.

The box contained papers and parchments, which he hastily threw upon the table. "Nothing but papers," he muttered, and laughed bitterly. "My mother and sisters cannot live upon them."

He was about to throw the papers back into the box when a feeling of curiosity prompted him to open one of them. He was surprised to see it was written in English, a language he fortunately could read with ease. "I wonder how my father got these papers?" he thought to himself. "So far as I know, he never had anything to do with an English house." He began to read at first from mere curiosity, but he soon began to take a lively interest in their contents. He read on and on: took up first one paper, and then another: and in his great eagerness did not notice that his candle was nearly burnt out, till its flame shot up, flickered for a moment, and then died out.

"How vexatious!" exclaimed Augustine, "just when a ray of hope had appeared to me—just when I saw my way to help my mother—to be thus left in darkness. I must see if I can find a bit of candle elsewhere." He groped his way to the kitchen, and felt about everywhere, but without finding what he wanted. "Well," he said to himself, "I must have patience till morning comes, and the night will give me time to think over what I have read."

He gathered the papers together in the dark, put them back carefully into the box, which he re-locked, and then took it upstairs to his own room. Then he threw himself upon his bed, and thought long before his eyes closed in sleep. As he slept he had a pleasant, hopeful dream. He fancied himself in a distant land, in the midst of a dense forest of gigantic trees; he moved forward with difficulty; from time to time broad streams, steep rocks, and thorny bushes stopped his path, and wild beasts glared at him through the thickets. His heart failed him, but suddenly the terrors of the scene vanished, and he was standing on a beautiful flowery plain, watered by clear streams, and lighted by golden sunshine. Precious stones grew on the flower-stalks, instead of flowers, beautiful birds flew overhead, and butterflies flitted from flower to flower. Augustine tried to catch them, but as he stretched out his hand towards the diamond flowers, whose brightness almost blinded him, he awoke.

"What a strange dream!" he thought, as he awoke. "I wonder how it came into my head! Ah, it was those papers," he exclaimed aloud; "they must have caused it; now let me read them again."

He dressed himself hastily, and then opened the box, half of whose contents he had already read. After reading them all through most carefully, he fell into a reverie. "Strange indeed!" he said to himself. "These papers may prove a mine of wealth to us, if circumstances have not greatly changed. I must find that out, and then —I am resolved—but first I must tell my mother about it."

He got up, took the papers, and found his mother, who was about her usual household work.

"Mother," he said, "did you know my father had a brother?"

"O yes, certainly; his name was Richard: he went away from home when he was only eighteen. Your father has often spoken to me about him. He had a restless unruly spirit, and after many strange adventures he entered the English army, and distinguished himself much, and was made an officer: he never returned home, but died in America. Ten or twelve years ago your father received this news, and also a tin box which I have never seen since. Your father must have put it aside, and forgot it."

"Then it is this same box I found yesterday, mother," said Augustine. "It contains some deeds, and a journal, and other things, which show Uncle Richard was by no means discontented with his lot. He appears to have been a distinguished officer, and if not a rich man, yet evidently he was never in want. Among his papers I have found this document, mother;" and he drew out and unfolded a large parchment. "It is in English, and signed by the governor of the English possessions in America. Its contents are a deed of gift to Captain Richard Stucker, of twenty thousand acres of land to him and his heirs for ever, as a reward for his services. The position of the land is minutely described, and its extent is as great as a German kingdom. Mother, this land belongs to us; for here is my uncle's will, signed on his death-bed, making my father his heir. What a happiness it will be for us, if this claim is valid, and we can take possession of this little kingdom!"

His mother shook her head doubtfully. "If," she said, "this deed were really worth anything, your father would never have thrown it aside thus. Do not build any hopes upon it, Augustine, for the disappointment would be painful to you."

"Dear mother, my hopes are not so deceitful as you fancy," Augustine answered, quickly. "This property in a distant country could have little or no value to my father, for he was a rich man. But how different it all is now! Poor as we are, I can see no opening for us in our native land; and, mother dear, it is a fearful thought for me that your old age may be one of troubles and privations. Whereas, if I set out for this fruitful land, and make good our claims to it from my uncle's will, then I can take you to a happy home, and a future full of bright hopes! Dear mother, it will be such a happiness for me, if I can lighten your heart and remove your anxieties. If I succeed in that I shall be the happiest man on earth."

"My good son!" said his mother, through her tears. "What a blessing your love is to me! But, Augustine, you forget what dangers and difficulties you must encounter, if you carry out your scheme. You, so young and inexperienced, what would you do, even if your hopes were fulfilled, and your claims acknowledged? Would you settle in a fearful solitude, and pass your whole future life in the wilderness? Augustine, I cannot bear to think of it!"

"O mother!" he exclaimed, "what prospects are there for me in Germany? Without means to finish my studies, what is my future life likely to be? I shall remain a poor writer and copier, perpetually haunted by the thought that the fortune which had so unexpectedly offered itself had been thrown away through my cowardice. Let me at least try. We have nothing to lose, and may gain much."

His mother wavered, for she could not say her son was wrong. A poor prospect, indeed, seemed to be his in his native land; while perhaps in America he might, after a few years of hard work, secure a comfortable living. Her troubled heart must silence itself before such a hope for her boy.

"But the means!" she exclaimed, half-yielding, half-doubting; "where are the means for such a journey, and how are we to live in your absence? My dear son, your plan is impracticable."

"I have thought of all that, mother," he replied; "if we can sell this house we should receive such a sum for it that there would be both enough for my expenses, and sufficient for you all to live upon for the next two or three years—my absence would in no case last so long as that; and if I arrive safely in New York, I shall find help there, of which I have not yet told you. Uncle Richard has left two thousand dollars there—his savings—for my father and his heirs; and this will pay my travelling expenses and buy what we most need. Mother, Providence has showed me these papers which every one had forgotten, and I shall never be happy if I do not try to obtain this property; trust me, I will not set about this affair in a hasty, imprudent way."

"But, Augustine, the long voyage and all its dangers! I shall tremble for you at every gust of wind that blows."

Augustine laughed: "Mother, shall I not be in God's hands as much there as here? Not a hair can fall from my head without His permission: it is He whom the winds and waves obey. God will not forsake me. I should not dare to look forward to the future at all, if I did not trust in my Heavenly Father."

"Well," said his mother, conquered by her son's firm trust; "God will always help and bless so good a son; go, then, in peace, my boy. My prayers will be ever with you."

With a happy heart did Augustine then make his preparations. His chief care was for the comfort of his mother and sisters when he should be far away: no sacrifice seemed to him too great for their sakes. He had no fear for the success of his undertaking, for he trusted in his Heavenly Father with child-like faith. "What can hurt me," he said, "if God is my help and shield?" In this happy confidence all his preparations were made, and truly there did seem to be a blessing on all he undertook. Their house sold better than either he or his mother had dared to hope, and thus his greatest anxiety—a provision for his dear ones left behind—was lessened. The parting from his mother and sisters was sad indeed; yet he left them with a hopeful heart, while they found their best comfort in praying for him.

CHAPTER II.

AUGUSTINE arrived safely in the great trading city of Bremen, and at once made inquiries for the first ship bound to New York. In those days the trade between Germany and America was not nearly so brisk as it is now, so it was fortunate for Augustine that he was at once directed to the captain of a merchant ship which was to sail the next day. Augustine went to him and stated his wishes.

The captain was a fierce-looking old man with white hair, deeply-furrowed cheeks, and a sun-burnt complexion. He had keen-looking grey eyes under bushy, overhanging eyebrows, and his thin closed lips did not seem as if accustomed to speak friendly words. Yet Captain Steding was not a hard, harsh man. His rough outside hid a noble heart. He was sitting in a sea-side tavern, when Augustine entered and asked to speak to him.

"What do you want, young man?" he asked, gruffly.

"Captain," said Augustine, "I wish to go with you to America."

"Indeed!" said the captain, looking sharply at him. "Then we must settle with each other at once, young man; for the 'Carolina' will sail early to-morrow morning, if we have a favourable wind. Pay down the fare, eighty-five thalers, and then go on board."

"Eighty-five thalers!" exclaimed Augustine. He had never thought the voyage could cost so much: if he were to pay such a sum only one louis d'or would remain to him; and then how could he ever return, if his plans were to fail?

"Eighty-five thalers!" he repeated. "Cannot I go on easier terms? I would willingly work and make myself useful, if I need not pay so much."

Captain Steding shrugged his shoulders, as he said—"I am sorry; but the owner of the 'Carolina' fixes the fare, and I have no power to alter it: you must either pay the whole sum or stay on shore."

Augustine himself could see no other alternative, and tears came into his eyes, as he exclaimed—"My poor mother!" He did not know he had said those words aloud; but the captain heard them, and his interest was increased in Augustine.

"Listen," he said; "why do you wish to go to America? Tell me, if it is no secret; for I am well known at New York, and perhaps I may be able to give you good advice: you are young, and must not take it ill if an old man takes interest in you. I do not ask out of mere curiosity."

Augustine looked at the old sailor, and guessed at the kind heart hidden under a rough exterior, and he resolved to tell him his whole story.

Captain Steding listened attentively, and

then said, "Let me see those papers. I understand something about business, and can tell you if they are worth anything; for let me tell you, young man, it would be very foolish in you to go to America without sufficient reason."

Augustine, who always carried the papers about with him, showed them at once to the old man, who, after reading them carefully, remained for some time lost in thought. "These papers are of value," he said, at last. "The title to the land is good; and your uncle's will is plain. But these sort of affairs require time; and it certainly would be well if you could come with me and see after these things yourself, with the help I could give you. But then the passage money—there's the difficulty."

Captain Steding paused, and kept silence for a few minutes, Augustine waiting anxiously for the result of his thoughts. At last the old man jumped up, and said to him, "Listen, young man: I have taken a fancy to you, and I feel sure you must be good, when you take so much care of your mother, and are so anxious to maintain her in comfort; and old Steding would think it wrong not to try to help you. I have business on hand just now which will employ me for two or three hours: wait till I return, and then I will see what I can do. Walk about the harbour till I come back, but do not go far."

Augustine readily agreed, and walked slowly up and down the quay, watching, with much curiosity, all that was going on amongst the shipping. A seaport town was a new scene for him, and, for a while, as he watched ships being laden or unladen, he forgot his anxieties. Suddenly, he heard a loud cry of distress: he turned round and saw a servant-maid rushing about in most frantic grief, and crying loudly for help. The girl was pointing to the harbour, into which the child she had in charge had fallen. Augustine, who was a good swimmer, instantly took off his coat, and plunged into the water. He quickly seized the child, and held its head above water. In the meantime, other people had seen what had happened: a boat was hastily manned and pushed off, and Augustine and the child were taken into it. The child soon came to itself, and Augustine was just about to walk away, when a well-dressed man rushed down to the quay, and seized the child in his arms.

"Does it live?" he exclaimed. The child looked up in his face, and smiled, and the father fervently thanked God for having spared his only child to him.

"And who saved its life?" he then inquired. The servant pointed to Augustine, whose hand he eagerly took. "Did you save my little Lucy?" he exclaimed; while a voice behind, which Augustine at once recognised to be Captain Steding's, added, "Great God, how wonderful are Thy ways, and how quickly hast Thou sent a reward to the good son! The child you have saved is my owner's little daughter: I was bringing him here to see you, just when you saved his only child from death. Herr Strootsof, this is the man you were about to help, who has now put you under an obligation."

Herr Strootsof, with tears in his eyes, thanked Augustine with heartfelt words. "Come with me," he then said; "and Steding, come also. I must go home, and my wife must thank you for saving our child: let us make haste, lest my wife should have heard already what has happened."

Augustine would have excused himself on account of his wet clothes; but Captain Steding cried, "Come along! I will answer for it Herr Strootsof will provide you with a change of clothes." Augustine gave in, thanking God in his heart, as he went, for having permitted him to save the life of a fellow-creature. In a few minutes they reached Herr Strootsof's house, and, thanks to the husband's haste, found his wife had heard nothing of the accident. As he told her what had happened, she became deadly pale, and covered her child with kisses, and then took Augustine's hand with a grateful look.

"You have saved our child's life," she said; "how shall we ever repay you for it?"

"Oh, say nothing about that," said Augustine, hastily; "I have only done what any one else would have done in my place."

"At any rate," interrupted Captain Steding, "you have made your clothes wet enough. Madam, will you permit me to find a change for him?" Eagerly was everything offered that Augustine could possibly want.

CHAPTER III.

Though Augustine's nature was too noble for him even to have thought of payment for the service he had done, yet, when Herr Strootsof offered him a free passage to America, and lots of recommendations, he gratefully accepted his kindness. His disinterestedness soon won confidence and esteem both from Captain Steding and the rich merchant. Herr Strootsof would have willingly kept Augustine with him for a time; but Captain Steding was anxious to sail at once, and Augustine thought every hour in Bremen so much lost time. Herr Strootsof and his wife showed him so much kindness, that he felt it hard to part with his new friends.

Early next morning he went on board the "Carolina;" an hour later the anchor was weighed, and she stood out to sea. Captain

Steding treated Augustine like a son, and made him share his own cabin, which was, of course, the best in the ship.

Augustine employed his time well during the long voyage. There was an American on board who could speak the Indian language with almost as much ease as his native tongue, and from him Augustine learned the language at Captain Steding's recommendation; as he reminded him that he would be so much among the Indians, that it would be of the greatest possible use to him to be able to speak and understand their language. Augustine took the captain's advice, and many a long hour was spent in study with Nathaniel Cooper—or Natty, as he was usually called—with much mutual pleasure and benefit. The two became the best of friends, greatly to Captain Steding's satisfaction, for he knew Natty was a good and brave man.

The voyage to New York was unusually long, for they had constant baffling winds,

c

so that they had been nearly three months at sea before they sighted America.

It was with great delight that Augustine saw the distant land, which opened such rich hopes to him. He could not conceal his joy from Natty, who answered him so shortly that Augustine remarked it, and exclaimed,

"What is the matter, Natty? Are you not glad to see land at last? I thought you would be especially glad, because America is your native country."

"It is," said Natty, sighing; "but——"

"But what?" said Augustine. "You have something on your mind, Natty; tell me what it is."

Natty answered, hesitatingly, "I am glad enough to see my native country; but when I reach it, I shall have a loss the thought of which troubles me greatly."

"And what is it?" repeated Augustine.

"What else but parting with you," cried Natty. "I love you truly. I have no relations living—no father, mother, brothers, or sisters. I stand alone in the world, and I am about to be separated from the only man I really love. Is not that sad enough? If I only were rich and independent I would never leave you."

"But, Natty," cried Augustine, joyfully, "why need we part, when it would grieve me as much as you to do so? Stay with me, Natty. You know what my prospects are. Throw in your lot with mine, and let us work and hope together."

"It cannot be," replied Natty, hastily. "You are rich, and I am poor; you are a well-educated man, and I am only a common sailor—a squatter's son. No, no, Augustine: you would soon be tired of me."

"Natty," exclaimed Augustine, "I am not such an ungrateful fellow as to forget all you have done for me. O Natty! will you not trust your friend? And if I am richer than you are (which will only be if my hopes are fulfilled), you shall share it all with me; and now you can give me your help and your advice, which will be of more value to me than thousands of acres of land. O Natty! share with me all, good and bad fortune, or whatever God may send."

Natty listened in silence. He had not thought before of the great use he might be to his friend: he knew how to cut down trees, to build log-houses, to plant and reap; he was a good hunter, he understood Indian ways and manners; in short, the knowledge he had gained, as a squatter's son, would be invaluable to Augustine. "It is a good thought of yours," he said; "though I have no money, I have a good pair of arms to work for you. As you know, I once lived in the backwoods, and I found then that the Indians are not so bad as they are said to be; but when my father died, I left the country and took to a seafaring life. But now it is all changed again. It will make me a happy man to go with you, and you shall find me a true friend."

Augustine was delighted. "How glad I am," he answered: "if you are with me, I shall have new confidence for the future: all must go well while we are together."

Natty was about to answer, when another thought crossed his mind, which kept him silent in dismay.

"What is the matter now?" inquired Augustine.

"Why," he replied, "I have only just remembered how completely we are reckoning without our host. I cannot leave the ship till after her return to Europe."

"Why not?"

"Because I have pledged my word not to do so."

"But might not Captain Steding release you from your engagement?" returned Augustine.

"Oh, if he only would!" replied Natty; "but he could not if he would, unless Herr Strootsof had given leave to do so."

"And that is just what he has done, young man!" exclaimed a voice behind him, and a hand was placed on Natty's shoulder; he turned round and saw Captain Steding close beside him.

"Well, young man," he repeated, laughing at Natty's evident confusion: "for Augustine's sake I have the power to release you from your promise; and I am glad that all has happened just as I expected. Do not take it ill, my children, that I came softly behind you when I saw you talking together so eagerly, and that I have heard all you said. It was all for your good, so you must forgive me. I have long known, Natty, that you were a good, honest fellow, so I asked you to teach Augustine Indian; and I was pleased to see how soon you took to each other like brothers. It has all happened just as I wished, so I give you leave to go with Augustine, as Herr Strootsof allowed me to do; and, that you may not be penniless, he has given me a thousand thalers in charge for you, that you may buy a piece of land and settle near Augustine. Good luck to you both! and don't forget to keep a place by your fireside for old Captain Steding, when he has grown too old for a seafaring life."

Augustine and Natty were, indeed, overjoyed by this most unexpected kindness: they knew not how to express their gratitude.

"Ah, my children!" the old man exclaimed; "I see I was right, and that you deserve it all. Only keep true to each other, and be God-fearing, honest men, and then God will bless you wherever you go. Now I must leave you, for we are nearing the shore, and I must be at my post."

Captain Steding hurried away, and left the two young men together to talk over their plans. They were now fast approaching the shore, and soon the "Carolina" entered the harbour and cast anchor. This done, Captain Steding laid down his speaking-

trumpet, and said to the two young men:—
" Are you ready to land? Augustine, do not forget the letter Herr Strootsof gave you: the man to whom it is addressed will give you all the help you want, when he sees Herr Strootsof's handwriting. Come along."

Augustine hastened to follow Captain Steding's advice, and in a few minutes he and Natty found themselves in the heart of the flourishing town of New York.

CHAPTER IV.

ONE glorious summer's morning, two young men were walking together through a dense forest in America. Though the day was cloudless, yet not one ray of sunshine pierced through the thick foliage over the travellers' heads. The graceful maples with their hanging boughs, the stately oaks and elms, and the beautiful lime trees, interlaced their branches overhead. There was deep silence around, only broken by the faint sound of a gentle breeze, and the sweet songs of the birds; now and then the woodpecker's shrill cry might be heard, as it ran up and down the trunk of a half-dead tree, and stripped off its bark to find insects underneath.

The general stillness seemed strongly to impress the wanderers, for they only spoke to each other in whispers, while their eyes rested with fresh wonder and admiration on the scene around. The two young men were armed with rifles, and each had a hunting-knife in his belt. Before them walked a man equally well armed, and also carrying a tomahawk, which, with his strange dress and his dark skin, showed him to be an Indian. He was acting as guide to the others, a guide being indispensable through the dense forests.

It will easily be guessed who these two young men were. Augustine, thanks to Herr Strootsof's letters of recommendation, had had his rights acknowledged without difficulty. All the money due to him he caused to be paid over to Herr Strootsof's agent for the present, with the exception of the small sum he required for present necessities. His property was many days' journey from New York; so he hired the Indian we have just named as his guide, and was now, accompanied by Natty, making his way to his new home. Herr Strootsof's agent had strongly recommended him to make friends with the neighbouring Indians. If they succeeded in doing this, he was told, he had nothing to fear; for, savage and blood-thirsty as the Indians were said to be, they had never been known to break a treaty of peace.

The morning was far advanced when the Indian, who had till then walked on before them in silence, suddenly stopped, put down his weapons, and quietly seated himself under an oak.

"Why do you stop?" asked Augustine. "The day is not half over; are you tired or hungry, Dacotah?"

The Indian laughed contemptuously. "Dacotah can travel many days without being tired or hungry," he replied: "we have arrived at our journey's end."

"But where is the lake of which you spoke?" inquired Augustine.

The Indian silently pointed towards the west.

"Can it be there?" asked Augustine, doubtfully. "I can see nothing but trees and bushes all around us."

"An Indian is never mistaken in such matters," answered Natty. "Let us walk in that direction."

With some difficulty they forced their way through the thick underwood, and then all at once found themselves on the shore of a broad lake, which shone like gold in the bright sunlight. The view which opened before them was so wonderfully beautiful that, at first, neither Natty nor Augustine could speak for astonishment. The lake stretched far away, bordered by overhanging woods, which were here and there intersected by rich strips of pasture land; and over all was a cloudless sky, which completed the beauty of the picture.

"How glorious!" Augustine at last exclaimed, after a long silence; "and is this the place in which my future life is to be passed? But suppose Dacotah has deceived us, Natty? it would be hard indeed to tear ourselves away to seek a less beautiful spot."

"There can be no mistake," Natty replied. "Without doubt this is the lake of which we have been told. It is no delusion, Augustine: this is your own property, and heartily do I rejoice that it is so beautiful."

"It is paradise!" exclaimed Augustine. "How happy my mother and sisters will be when they see it. Natty, we must build our huts where we now stand."

"Yes," said Natty: "we need fear no want here. Dacotah says the lake abounds in fish, and the woods with game; the land, too, is evidently fruitful, and I see a clear brook close to us, so we have everything we can require for food. Now to make friends with the Indians, which is all-important; for you must not bring your mother here till that is done."

"But you forget the English fort we left only two hours ago," Augustine suggested: "will not that be sufficient protection for us?"

"You do not know the red men," Natty answered: "before we had any idea they were near us, they might be upon us; all resistance would be vain, and help would come too late. No, no, Augustine; you must smoke the pipe of peace with these Indians before it will be possible to settle here. Come, let us go back to Dacotah, and send him with a friendly message to his tribe; then, if they will receive us among them, you must give them the presents you have brought with you, and they will gladly give up this land to you in exchange. Do not fear, Augustine: we shall succeed in making friends with the red men."

The two young men then went back to Dacotah, who was still sitting under the oak.

"Listen, Dacotah," said Augustine; and then he proceeded to explain what they wanted. Dacotah got up at once, and said, "Dacotah is going. He will explain to the Delaware chief what the white men wish; if they come with open hands they will be welcome."

"Are you going alone?" asked Augustine; "may not we go with you?"

"Dacotah will go and speak first," answered the Indian: "if the white men will be welcome, he will return to them before the sun has gone down behind the water."

He left them without another word, and quickly disappeared in the forest.

"Let us sit down," said Natty; "for we must not go far before Dacotah returns."

They put down their rifles, and then threw themselves on the moss at the foot of the oak, and began to talk of Dacotah's embassy and of their plans for the future. But soon Natty gave Augustine a sign for silence, and pointed to a part of the wood from whence a stately stag was slowly moving towards them without suspecting danger.

"He will be a glorious prize if he comes

a little nearer," whispered Natty: "take a good aim, Augustine; if you are to live in this country you must learn to be a good shot." Augustine took aim. The stag came nearer; he fired, and, after one bound forwards, the stag fell dead.

The young men sprang up, but they had only taken a few steps forward when the bushes seemed to move, and a tall young Indian, armed with bow and arrows and a tomahawk, stood before them. He stopped when he saw the white men, and exclaimed "Ugh!" Then he laid his hand on his tomahawk and brandished it over his head. Augustine and Natty were hardly less surprised to see the young Indian; they faced him for a while in silence, till at last the Indian stepped back for a pace or two, and leant against a large tree.

"He is a Delaware Indian," whispered Natty; "we must try to make friends with him."

Augustine then quickly broke off a green

bough, put down his rifle, and walked up to the young Indian, who scowled upon him fiercely. Natty had his rifle ready cocked in his hand, to show that any attack on Augustine would be at once avenged. The Indian did not move a limb, but looked like a statue of red stone, as Augustine went up to him with the green bough in his hand.

"We are the red man's friends," said Augustine; "we come with no bad intentions," he added, smiling, as he offered his hand to the Indian. "Will my brother smoke the pipe of peace with me?"

"What business has the white man in the Delaware's hunting-ground?" answered the Indian. "Why must he come over the salt water to steal Wenonda's prey? Wenonda has followed this stag ever since the sun appeared on the mountain-tops, and was just about to seize his prey. White men can never be friends with the red men; the tomahawk cannot be buried."

"But I will give up this stag to my

brother," Augustine answered, gently; "the stag is yours; I give up all claim to it."

"Begone!" said the Indian, angrily; "Wenonda will not take what has been stolen from him as a gift. Wenonda is a mighty hunter: he will follow another stag, and will have nothing to do with the white man. The white man's rifle has been fired on the Delaware's hunting-ground, and the Delaware will be avenged. Wenonda and the white men never can be friends."

Augustine again tried to appease the young Indian's wrath, and told him that the ground on which he had shot the stag was his own.

But this only enraged him more. "White men are snakes," he cried; "they creep into the Indians' wigwams, and poison them with fire-water. If the white man takes the Indians' hunting-ground, let him beware; Wenonda will kill him, and take his scalp."

Augustine was about to reply, but Wenonda stopped him: "Wenonda's ears are closed," he said: "the young chief will not listen to the serpent hissing."

Then, with a haughty look of defiance, he again brandished his tomahawk, and would, without doubt, have made use of it, if Natty had not pointed his rifle at him: caution made him pause. Natty guessed his feelings, and the inextinguishable hatred that had been awakened. He knew Indian ways, and he dreaded the after results of this ill-omened meeting. "Augustine," he said, "I must shoot this fellow."

"No, no!" he replied, in horror.

The Indian looked fixedly at Natty; and, though he could not understand the words that had been spoken, he evidently guessed their purport; for he shook his tomahawk menacingly at Natty, and the next moment disappeared among the bushes. Natty was about to follow, but Augustine stopped him, and gently took his rifle from him. "Enough," he cried; "let him go; he will reflect afterwards that I shot the stag with no intention of disputing his right to it."

"We shall see," returned Natty: "for my

part, I believe he will for the future be our bitterest enemy; he will never forgive us for taking his prey from him. I should be easier if I had sent a bullet through his head."

"O Natty, what sinful words!" Augustine exclaimed, reprovingly; "I would rather have remained in poverty all my life than gain my rights through murder."

"Well," returned Natty, rather scornfully, "you must force your tender conscience into silence, if you are to live near these wild Indians."

"Never! never!" exclaimed Augustine; "I would rather suffer anything than do that; and, after all, Natty, that young Indian was not so very far wrong. The white people have often injured the natives cruelly, as you yourself have told me; and we can hardly now expect them to receive us with open arms. Let us see if we cannot soften them by kindness and Christian love."

"It will be a long business," answered Natty, drily; "in the meantime we must be on our guard, or this young fellow will play us a trick. But never mind, Augustine—there is no use in talking about it; let us look at the stag you have killed, for we will not throw him away because the Indian will not have him. See what a fine fellow he is! You will be a good hunter in time: this is a promising beginning. Now help me to cut up this beast, and then we will light a fire and cook part of it: we will keep part for Dacotah."

The young men set to work, forgetting all about their late encounter with the Indian; but they were soon to be reminded of him. Natty was stooping down to cut a slice of venison, when something whistled through the air, and the next moment an arrow stuck in the tree above him.

"That was meant for me," exclaimed Natty, as he seized his rifle, and pushed his way through the thicket. The next moment his rifle went off. Natty returned almost directly.

"Missed!" he exclaimed, angrily. "There was no use in following the fellow; but now you see, Augustine, what we have to expect: he will never rest till he has killed us both."

"Unless we succeed in softening him," replied Augustine. "His heart may not be so hard as to withstand true love and kindness. I will not give him up, but shall hope to make friends with him at last."

"It would have been far better if I had shot him," retorted Natty. "After his attack upon me he deserved nothing better than to be shot down like a wild beast."

"O Natty!" said Augustine, reproachfully; "does not the Bible say, 'Love your enemies, bless them that curse you, and pray for them that despitefully use you.' Let us forgive this wild Indian for his wicked deed; he does not know what he does, for his mind has never been enlightened by the truth; I shall hope better things of him in time; perhaps one day he will be as true a friend to us as he is now a bitter enemy."

Though Natty was a good man, he did not agree with Augustine. He had not learned that true Christian charity which bears everything, after Christ's example. He looked upon the Indians as little better than wild animals, who might be swept away from the face of the earth if they stood in his way. So he now looked at Augustine with surprise, shrugged his shoulders, and answered, shortly, "When you know these Indians better, you will think differently; in the meantime, help me in what we were doing."

In half-an-hour they had lighted a bright fire, and Natty had made a spit of a straight piece of wood, on which they roasted the venison. Their meal finished, and their thirst quenched from the clear spring of which we have spoken, they sat down to await Dacotah's return.

CHAPTER V.

The evening was drawing on when Dacotah appeared, and told the result of his mission. "The Delaware chief bids the white man welcome," he said. "The pipe of peace is filled, and is ready to be smoked. Uncas has prepared a seat for the strangers who come over the salt water."

"Will Dacotah lead us to him to-day?" asked Natty.

"Yes," he replied.

"Then we are ready to follow," said Augustine. "But, first, my brother must eat; the white man's eye is sharp: he has killed a stag, and we have left some for Dacotah."

He smiled in return, and said, "My brother is good; he thinks of his absent friend. Dacotah thanks him." The Indian satisfied his hunger, and then told the young men to follow him.

"The sun is going down," he said; "before it has sunk behind the mountains, the white man must sit by the Delaware's fireside; Dacotah has promised it."

He moved on quickly, and the young men followed him.

After an hour's march they emerged from the forest, and saw the Indians' huts in front of them. In the centre of the village stood a hut, somewhat larger than the others, which Natty pointed out to Augustine.

Their guide went straight to it, while Augustine looked round curiously, having never seen an Indian village before. In front of the huts the women sat, the children played, and many of the warriors lay stretched at full length, eyeing the white men with no small curiosity; but they all looked friendly, and courteously returned the young men's greeting. Augustine and Natty entered the large hut, and saw the principal warriors assembled round the fire. Others then entered, and took their places, all greeting them silently. Uncas, the old chief, signed to them to take their seat by the fire. They obeyed in silence, waiting for the chief to speak; for Natty, who knew Indian habits well, had told Augustine to do so. Many a pair of dark eyes were fixed upon the young men, who bore their gaze so quietly as to make a good impression upon the assembled Indians.

At last Uncas said, "The white men are welcome; what do my brothers want from the Indian chief? His ears are open."

Augustine told what his wishes were. "The king of the white men has given me land; I am come to take possession. But if Uncas objects, let him speak." Uncas was silent for a while, as if weighing Augustine's words. Then he said, "My brother is welcome; the land is yours. Uncas will not hinder you from taking possession."

Augustine suppressed the exclamation of joy on his lips; for if he had shown his pleasure in words, he would have been despised by the Indians, who look upon self-command as the greatest of all virtues.

"Uncas is right," he said. "I desire your friendship. Will my brother accept a present from me?"

Without waiting for an answer he opened his hunting-bag, and took out a heap of beads, and other glittering toys, which he spread out before the Indians. The best he gave to the chief, and divided the rest among the other Indians, who received them with undisguised pleasure.

Uncas said, smiling, "The young white man is wise. The open-handed are always welcome; the red men will be his friends."

The pipe of peace was then handed to Uncas, who lighted it, took a few puffs, and then handed it to Augustine, who followed his example, and then passed it on to Natty. It made the round of the whole circle, and then the treaty of peace was considered to be concluded.

"My brothers are welcome," Uncas repeated. "The chief's wigwam stands open and ready to receive his friends. Uncas will give them maize and venison."

Augustine again thanked him, and the assemblage were just about to disperse, when a young warrior was seen at the door of the hut, staring at the white men. Natty started back, for he saw it was Wenonda, with whom they had had so unpleasant an encounter. The young Indian looked round on all present with anger, for he guessed what had just taken place.

"Wenonda, my son," said Uncas, pointing to the strangers: "these white men are our friends." Wenonda answered, haughtily, "Wenonda cannot be their friend: he hates the white men!"

There was a movement of surprise among the Indians; but Uncas remained, though he looked reproachfully at his son, as he said,

"The white men are under my protection. Wenonda must obey his father's commands. The pipe of peace has been smoked, and the tomahawk is buried."

Then he arose, and left the hut, signing to the white men to follow him. Wenonda dared not say more, but threw a glance of hatred at the strangers.

In the meantime, the sun had gone down, and the night was coming on. The two young men followed the chief to his wigwam, where food was set before them, and then they lay down together on the bearskin he assigned to them; but instead of sleeping, they whispered to each other of their hopes and fears.

"Wenonda's hatred is most unfortunate for us," said Natty. "We must not think of settling here till we have either put him out of the way, or appeased his wrath—the former will be easier to do than the latter. We should have shot him down in the wood, when he showed himself so bitter against us."

"No, no!" answered Augustine. "He will become gentle, when we show ourselves to be so. It is my great aim to win his affections, and I will leave no means untried to do so. No hatred is too great to be conquered by love."

Natty replied, 'You do not understand Indian natures, Augustine; their hatred is as inextinguishable as their friendship, when once gained, is firm. Beware of Wenonda! If he does not dare to show his enmity in public, he will murder us in secret. It must be a struggle for life or death; either he or we must die!"

"No," repeated Augustine, authoritatively. "No drop of his blood shall be shed. God's command is, 'Thou shalt not kill,' and I would rather die than break God's laws."

"Self-preservation is also a duty," urged Natty.

"It is, but it is a higher one to fulfil the law of love," replied Augustine. "Christ would not have saved the world, if He had thought as you do. He offered Himself for all mankind, and loved even those who crucified Him. Natty, we are not worthy to be His followers, if we do not try to imitate Him. No heart is too hard to be moved by love."

Natty was silent for awhile, and then seized Augustine's hand. "You are a good man," he said, with feeling. "Well, I will do as you wish: then at least, whatever happens, we shall have a clear conscience."

Augustine thanked him heartily, and added, "Let us hope and trust, Natty. My heart tells me that our endeavours will succeed at last."

CHAPTER VI.

However much Augustine might hope to soften Wenonda by kindness, his efforts seemed to be of little avail. Yet he resolved not to leave the village till he had made friends with the young man. Augustine would speak to him kindly, and give him presents, which Indians are usually most eager to receive; but Wenonda would turn from him in contemptuous silence, and either would refuse his presents, or take them and then trample them under his feet. If Augustine went out hunting, as he often did, and came home laden with game and venison, and laid the best pieces down before Wenonda's hut, he would throw them contemptuously to the dogs, and then laugh bitterly at the white man for his cowardly cunning in trying to bribe his foe, instead of fighting with him.

Augustine bore this treatment patiently, and would not relax his efforts. He found great pleasure in the friendship of the other Indians, especially in that of Uncas, whose guests he and Natty still were. But especially was he pleased by the affection shown him by Uncas' daughter, a girl of fourteen. The more Wenonda hated Augustine, the more did his gentle sister, Flittah, love him. From the first, she and Augustine became friends; and he it was who sowed the seed of Christian truth in her heart, and told her of the love of God, and of Christ having come into the world to save sinners. Flittah listened eagerly to his words, though Wenonda tried to prevent her doing so.

"Brother," she would say, "the white man is kind to me, and teaches me to love all men: why then should Flittah hate and shun him?"

"The white man is a snake, and is bewitching Flittah," he would answer, angrily. "Why has he come over the sea to rob us of our hunting-ground, and to steal our game? The white man hates Wenonda, and Wenonda will kill him. Wenonda is a brave warrior, and the white man is a dog!"

Then Flittah would leave her brother, and, flying to Augusine, tell him what Wenonda had said. "Do not provoke him," he would reply. "Wenonda does not know his white brother: if he could look into my heart he would think differently. Patience—Wenonda will become my friend in time."

Then Augustine would again try to soften Wenonda, but in vain: the gulf seemed only to widen between them; for Wenonda looked upon Augustine as a treacherous foe, who covered his evil intentions under a mask of friendship. It was difficult to struggle against so deep-rooted a hatred, but Augustine would not despair.

Many weeks passed thus. One day Wenonda disappeared, and Flittah answered Augustine's inquiries about him by saying he had gone out hunting, to lay up a store of food for the winter.

"If that is his intention," said Augustine, "I will help him. I will go out hunting at once." Flittah shuddered, and, hastily looking round to see no one was near, whispered to Augustine,—

"My brother must not leave Flittah till Wenonda returns: he does not want the white man's help. The white man must stay with Flittah, and tell her about the Good Spirit."

"I will do that when I return," replied Augustine; "but the warriors will take me for a woman, if I do not hunt with them."

"My brother must stay with Flittah," she repeated, anxiously; "for dangers lurk in the woods."

Augustine laughed. "I have often been in the woods," he replied, "and have met with no dangers there."

"The woods are dangerous," again said Flittah.

"If they are," said Augustine, "the Good Spirit will watch over me, and protect me."

"But my brother must stay with Flittah," she repeated: "the hunters will be jealous of the white men if they are more successful than they are. My brother must not go."

Augustine might, perhaps, have stayed, for he began to suspect there was some reason for Flittah's mysterious warning, had not Uncas entered the hut and decided the matter by saying, "My brother is right; the white man is a good shot, and will be a mighty hunter in time."

Flittah did not dare any longer to urge Augustine to stay, but she whispered to him, "My brother must be on his guard, for the Fierce Wolf is in the woods."

Augustine knew at once what she meant. Wenonda was called the Fierce Wolf; he had no doubt then that danger did threaten him. However, he would not change his intention, but put his trust in God.

He started early next morning with Natty, promising to return laden with game. By noon he had been so successful, that he thought of returning home. He called to Natty, but he did not hear, for he was chasing a stag at some distance. Augustine called many times, but received no reply, so he came to the conclusion Natty had returned home, and determined to follow his example.

He had hardly gone a hundred steps, when he came out in an open space in the wood. Some broken rocks were before him, shining bright in the sun; near them grew a gigantic old cork-tree: its trunk was hollow, and its whole aspect showed it had been struck by lightning, yet its lower branches were thickly covered with leaves, though the upper ones were quite dead. Augustine, as he looked at it, thought to himself, "What a hiding-place this would be for a panther!" A wild beast could, indeed, have easily concealed itself in the thick foliage of the lower branches. Suddenly Augustine heard a slight noise, which seemed to proceed from the bushes near him. Fancying a wild beast was near, he held his rifle ready to fire; when, all at once, he thought he saw a human form among the bushes. He instantly threw himself on the ground, just in time, for the same instant a shot was fired that would, had he been standing upright, have gone through his heart.

Augustine sprang up and took shelter behind an adjacent tree, muttering to himself, "No doubt it was the Fierce Wolf;" and, for the moment, indignation conquered his usual gentleness. The next moment he noticed a slight movement in the old tree near him, though the air was too still to stir a leaf. He looked again, and then silently pointed his rifle towards the tree, for the bright sunlight was glancing on a panther's spotted skin. The animal was evidently watching its victim, and that victim was to be Wenonda. For a moment Augustine hesi-

tated. If Wenonda had not attempted his life the instant before, he would have shot the panther at once. But he was not without human infirmities: he had only, he thought, to stand still, and his revenge would be executed—the only enemy he had in the world would be dead, and he might bring his mother in safety to America. The temptation was great, but Augustine's better nature triumphed over it. "No!" he said to himself; "we are taught to return good for evil." He took aim and fired just as the beast was in the act of springing. The panther gave one fearful cry, and the next moment fell dead on the ground: Augustine's shot had penetrated the brain.

"Ugh!" exclaimed Wenonda, in surprise. Without reloading, Augustine left his hiding-place and fearlessly went to the place from whence the voice proceeded; but Wenonda had disappeared.

"He is gone!" exclaimed Augustine, aloud; "is he softened by my having saved his life; or is it his dread of me which has driven him away?" He could not decide the question in his own mind; but the thought of having done a good deed, and returned good for evil, made him happy. All at once, he heard steps behind him; he turned round and saw Natty close beside him, who had hastened forward on hearing the report of his gun. Augustine pointed to the panther, and said he had just shot him; but he did not say a word about Wenonda. The friends returned together to the village, and were received by Flittah with the greatest joy. The death of the panther increased Augustine's fame as a mighty hunter amongst the Indians.

CHAPTER VII.

Who would not have thought that after Augustine had thus saved his life, Wenonda would have forgotten his hatred in return? But it was not so. After a few days' absence, Wenonda returned to the village; but it was not to show gratitude to his preserver, for he looked at him as fiercely as ever, and would not answer when he spoke to him. This troubled Augustine greatly, for he had hoped for better things; but it only strengthened his determination not to leave the country till he had made friends with Wenonda. Augustine determined to be patient, and in the meantime to strengthen his friendship with the other Indians. It was not difficult to do so, for they already loved the white man for his courage and generosity, and admired him as a mighty hunter. Uncas, in particular, gave him every proof of affection. But what we are about to relate increased to the highest degree their attachment to Augustine.

A deadly fever broke out in the village, such as usually swept away half its inhabitants. Uncas was the first seized by it, and Flittah's tears fell fast as she sat by her father's bedside. Their native "medicine men" were sent for, but they could do no good; still less the wise men, who professed to charm away disease. Uncas appeared to be at the point of death. Augustine was then absent on a hunting expedition; when he returned, he found Flittah sitting on the ground in tears.

"What has happened to my sister?" Augustine exclaimed. "Why do you cry thus bitterly?"

"Uncas is dying," replied the child, through her tears.

"Uncas dying?" repeated Augustine. "Take your white brother to him at once;

perhaps he may know how to cure the chief."

Flittah looked up joyfully. "Is my brother, then a medicine man?" she inquired, eagerly.

"Yes," said Augustine, rejoicing at the thought his knowledge of medicine might now prove of great use.

Flittah instantly led him to Uncas' wigwam. Augustine examined the sick man carefully, and then said to Flittah, "Be comforted, my sister; before the sun has gone down, your father's fever will have left him."

Then he hastened into the woods, and gathered there certain roots, of whose virtues in such cases he was well aware. From them he made a cooling drink, which he gave to the sick man, who, in a few hours, became evidently better. Augustine watched by him to note every change. His constant care and skill were rewarded with success. Before the sun had gone down, the fever had left Uncas; his eye was clear, his senses had returned; he had only weakness now to contend with. Augustine's fame spread rapidly from mouth to mouth; he was treated by all with the deepest respect, as a wonderful "medicine man."

Wenonda alone remained as cold and forbidding as before. But soon fever showed itself in him also; his eyes burned, his knees trembled. He concealed it as long as possible, and rejected the remedies Augustine offered with contempt. But fever soon obtained the mastery, and then Augustine watched over him with the same anxious care as over Uncas.

"You are a fool," Natty said. "Now that you could so easily leave this man to his fate, you must forsooth put forth all your powers to save him. Augustine, you are acting like an idiot."

But Augustine only increased his care, and said, quietly, "If I were to let any one die whose life it was in my power to save, I should be a murderer. It is my duty to do my best; no fears shall deter me. Christ commands us to love our enemies and to do them good."

Natty was touched, and replied, "In men's eyes you are a fool; but God, who sees men's hearts, does not think so."

Augustine merely smiled in reply, then again felt the sick man's pulse, gave him a cooling drink, and moistened his lips with water. Wenonda also, in time, recovered, yet still he showed no gratitude. He left the village, and remained in the woods for whole days together. Natty blamed him bitterly; but Augustine only said, "'Judge not, and ye shall not be judged.' Though I am grieved that I have not touched Wenonda's heart, yet I do not regret what I have done."

Many more Indians were attacked, but, thanks to Augustine's skill and care, none of the cases proved fatal. His fame had now spread so far, that one day a message came to him from the chief of the Pequod Indians, to beg the white man to visit his village to drive away the same terrible fever. Against Natty's advice, he at once consented to return with the messenger to his village, which was distant a day's journey. The chief's son was lying dangerously ill. Augustine was able to save his life, and that of several of the other Indians. Nothing could exceed the gratitude shown him for his services. The Indians wished to load him with presents; they brought to him their rings and their bracelets—they laid the game they had killed before his wigwam; but Augustine would accept nothing, and only begged for their friendship. The chief then offered to adopt him as his son; but this too, Augustine refused, telling the chief that he had a mother and sisters for whose welfare he must care; he further told him that he hoped eventually to settle in the neighbourhood, and that it was only his fear of Wenonda which prevented his doing so at once. The news that he was going to be their neighbour greatly delighted the Indians.

Then followed threats against Wenonda, and Augustine had to exert all his influence to prevent his new friends breaking out into hostilities against him and his tribe. At last, all the sick having entirely recovered, Augustine wished to return to his old friends, and asked the Pequod chief to let him have a guide through the forest.

The chief was ready to comply with all Augustine's wishes, but he first assembled all his warriors, that they might solemnly return thanks to the great medicine man. The fire was lighted, the warriors sat round it in a circle, and Augustine took the place of honour beside the chief. The pipe of peace went round, and then the chief stood up, and spoke thus to Augustine: "My brother is a mighty enchanter. He has come over the salt water to fight the bad spirits, who tried to kill my bravest warriors. The white man is wise, and he is good. The Pequods thank him for his help, and desire his friendship. My brother, the Pequods will never fight against you. The tomahawk is for ever buried between us! If my brother wants help, the Pequods will come to his aid. Our warriors are ready to protect him, and to die for him. My brother must hear our words, for they are true. We love the white man; the good Spirit will be angry, if we ever forget what he has done for us."

The warriors then got up, and addressed Augustine in the same strain. Augustine made a suitable answer, and the assembly was just about to disperse, when a white man hastily entered the circle. It was Natty: he looked very pale, and spoke hurriedly to the astonished Augustine, who was much disturbed by what he said.

"This is bad news, indeed," he said; "if Wenonda continues to hate me thus, I dare not return to his village; but happily there are friends here that will help us."

Then, turning to the Indians, he said, as

he led Natty forward, "This man is my friend; he puts himself under the protection of the brave Pequods: if they love me, they will smoke the pipe of peace with him."

"The medicine man's friend is welcome," the chief replied.

"My friends," continued Augustine: "I and my friend seek the Pequods' protection—we dare not return to the Delaware village."

"The white men are welcome," repeated the chief. "Have the Delawares injured our friend's friend?"

"The Delawares are true men," replied Augustine; "but the Fierce Wolf prowls in the woods, and thirsts for the blood of the white men, who have done him no harm. My friend had killed a bear, and the Fierce Wolf tried to take it from him. He said, "The white men are dogs: they have no right to hunt in the Delawares' hunting-ground. They must go to the Pequods, if they want to hunt bears." My friend struggled with the Fierce Wolf, but he wounded him with his tomahawk, and my friend was obliged to fly. He is here; and here," he said, as he uncovered Natty's shoulder, "is the bite of the Fierce Wolf."

A cry of anger broke from the assembled warriors. "My friend shall not be chased from the Delawares' wigwams like a dog," the chief exclaimed. "The Pequods are brave, and will avenge the medicine man and his friend."

This speech was received with applause, and all were at once in movement. One of the warriors went up to a dwarf oak, that grew in front of the hut, and stripped off its bark; another cut off its branches with his tomahawk, and left it naked and bare. A third daubed it with a blood-red colour; then the other warriors danced round it, singing a strange wild song.

"What does all this mean?" asked Augustine.

"It means," replied Natty, "that the Pequods are going to make war on the

Delawares, to avenge our cause. In truth, though I hate bloodshed, I am glad enough that Wenonda is going to be punished."

Augustine started: *he* had no wish for revenge, and with grief he reflected on the danger that through his means threatened his old friends, who were not to be blamed for Wenonda's misdoings. He tried to stop the Pequods; but, now that their warlike feelings had been aroused, that was quite out of his power. The chief now appeared in his war-paint, his two sons by his side, and was received with loud shouts by his warriors, who had in the meantime hacked the dwarf oak to pieces; he made a sign for silence, and then a short council was held, after which the warriors formed in line, headed by their chief.

Vainly did Augustine try once more to stop them. "The Delawares are innocent," he said, imploringly: "shall a whole tribe suffer for the fault of one of its members?" The chief gave no answer: the march was begun in silence.

"But," persisted Augustine, "it is a sin and shame to fall thus upon defenceless men."

"The Pequods are not snakes!" replied the chief; "a swift messenger has been sent to the Delawares with a bunch of arrows, whose tips are steeped in blood. The Delawares will be prepared."

Augustine saw he was but wasting words, he therefore armed himself hastily and followed the Indians, hoping, at least, to be able to avert mischief, and to shield the innocent.

CHAPTER VIII.

NIGHT came on when the journey was half over, and a halt was called. Moss and underwood were cleared away, and then a fire was lighted, round which some of the warriors lay, while others kept watch. Their rest was not disturbed, and at dawn of day the march was continued. They were about a league from the village when the party halted at a sound from the chief, like the cry of an owl; a second similar cry brought the principal warriors to his side. Augustine and Natty were with them, and saw, with surprise, that the Delaware warriors were drawn up on a clear space of ground, not one hundred paces distant. A short parley followed, the result of which Augustine watched with the deepest anxiety. He dreaded every moment to see the Pequods fall upon the Delawares; but it was not to be so.

The Pequods fell back, while their chief walked forward alone, the Delaware chief, Uncas, meeting him with a green bough in his hand; he spoke thus:—" The Pequod chief has sent a herald to the Delawares; he has dug up the tomahawk, and armed his warriors. But, Uncas does not wish peace to be broken; the red men should not shed each other's blood for slight causes. The Delawares are brave, and do not fear to fight; but they are also just, and justice is better than violence! Why does my brother wish for war?"

The Pequod chief was silent for a time, as if weighing what Uncas had said; then he replied,—" Uncas is a brave chief, for many scalps hang in his wigwam; he is wise, also. The Pequods do not wish for the Delawares' blood; but the Fierce Wolf has howled in the woods, and bitten the Pequods' friend."

"The Fierce Wolf is caught," Uncas replied, with such wonderful self-command that only a slight trembling of his lips betrayed his feelings. "He is here. That the Fierce Wolf is bad, is no reason why innocent blood should be shed. Brother, take the Fierce Wolf: he is yours."

Uncas made a signal, and some of his Indians came forward from the rear, leading Wenonda, whose hands were tied, but who looked as fierce and haughty as of old. He did not look at his father, who stood in silent sorrow, well knowing the horrible fate that awaited his son. At a sign from Mahtoree, the Pequod chief, he was received by his warriors as a prisoner, and taken to the rear.

"Uncas is a great chief," said Mahtoree; "his head is wise, and his heart is true. The Pequods and Delawares are friends; the tomahawk is buried; Mahtoree will lead his warriors back to their homes." He and Uncas then silently saluted each other, and the Delawares returned to their village. Augustine longed to follow them, for Uncas conduct had filled him with admiration; yet he felt he could hardly, under the circumstances, expect a very friendly reception, and, moreover, he still hoped to save Wenonda, which reason determined him to remain with the Pequods. They all marched back to their village. Augustine spoke to Wenonda, but he returned no answer, so he then turned to Natty to inquire what his fate would be; but Natty could give him no information. Then he asked Mahtoree the same question; but he only answered, "The white man will see; the Pequods will avenge the medicine man. Mahtoree is a great chief, and the strangers are under his protection." This was all Augustine could learn, so he remained in painful uncertainty.

Late at night the village was reached; Wenonda was taken to the chief's hut, where he was carefully watched. Augustine, who was very weary, went at once to rest, and did not awake till late the next morning. He found Natty was gone, so he rose in haste. As

he left his hut he was astonished to find the village deserted; no living creature was to be seen; all was still and silent.

Augustine hastened to the chief's hut: it was empty. "Oh," he thought, in horror, "if they should have put Wenonda to death!" Just then he thought he heard faint sounds from a part of the wood where he knew a space had been cleared. He hurried to the spot, and as he approached could distinguish voices; he hastened forward and saw before him a crowd of women and children on one side of the open space; on the other all the warriors were collected, full armed, and their war-paint on. He forced his way through them, and then saw a sight which made his blood run cold. Wenonda was before him, bound so tightly with thongs to a tree that he could not move his head. At a little distance stood a number of young warriors, who were laughing at him, and threatening him, and brandishing their tomahawks over their heads. One of them was just about to throw his at Wenonda, when he was stopped by a loud cry from Augustine. They paused for a moment in their fearful game, while he went up to Mahtoree, who was standing near. Natty was standing by, and Augustine asked him hastily, "What does this mean?"

"Wenonda is going to be punished," Natty answered, gravely; "his courage is to be tried, as you see, and then he will be burnt. It is a cruel punishment, but he deserves it."

"It shall not be!" cried Augustine: "he is a heathen, and knows no better: we might have done the same in his place; then think of his poor father!"

"Think what you are doing," said Natty: "the Indians will only turn upon you, if you rob them of their prey."

"Let them," returned Augustine: "I shall never know a happy hour again if I cannot stop them."

He then hastily approached Wenonda, and took out his knife. The Pequods shouted joyously, supposing Augustine wished to be the first to strike. Wenonda thought so also, and said, calmly and contemptuously, "The white man is a dog; he would not dare to touch Wenonda if he were not bound."

Without answering, Augustine cut the thongs which bound him, and said, "Wenonda is free: the white man loves even his enemies, and does not thirst for their blood. Return to your father."

The greatest surprise was shown by Wenonda, not unmixed with a softer feeling. He looked at Augustine, instead of making his escape. "Go," he repeated; "the path is open: let the Fierce Wolf save himself."

Wenonda started, as if wakened from a trance; he would then have fled, but it was too late. The Pequods were prepared, and he was, in a few minutes, recaptured, and once more tied to the tree. Augustine turned eagerly to Mahtoree to beg Wenonda's life.

"It cannot be," he answered, sternly;

"my white brother has been injured by the Fierce Wolf, and his friends must avenge him."

"But," he replied, "I do not wish for vengeance. With my whole heart do I forgive the Fierce Wolf, so you have no excuse for killing him: he has never injured you."

"The white man is too gentle," replied Mahtoree; "he can cure sick men, but he cannot avenge himself. Mahtoree's warriors have their tomahawks ready, and the Fierce Wolf must show he is brave. Go, brother: my ears are closed."

"Then open them again," cried Augustine. "Let Mahtoree and his warriors remember that it was I who saved them from death. You would have given me rewards, but I refused them all. Let the Pequods now show that they are thankful as well as brave: I, who have saved the lives of so many of your tribe, only ask this man's life in return. You cannot refuse me."

"The Pequods are grateful," answered

Mahtoree. "Let my brother take what he wishes from us; but the Fierce Wolf belongs to us alone: he must show if he is a man."

For one moment Augustine thought of threatening to send a pestilence amongst them, if they refused what he asked; but his nature recoiled from such a lie, though he knew it would have been effectual, as the Indians believed him to be an enchanter. Another expedient occurred to him. He rushed up to Wenonda, and threw his arms round him: then, turning to the Indians, he cried, "The Fierce Wolf is mine: the Pequods must kill me before they shall touch him: let them kill me if they will, but if they do they will murder the man who saved them from death."

Angry cries followed the bold words; tomahawks were raised, and Augustine believed his last hour was come. But at a sign from Mahtoree the tumult ceased as suddenly as it had begun. Augustine went on: "If the Pequods kill me, their name will become a reproach. All the red men will say the Pequods are worse than dogs, for dogs are thankful for kindness." A breathless silence ensued, then Mahtoree answered, " My white brother is right : the Pequods' name shall not be a reproach in the land."

Augustine's face was bright with joy, as he saw the warriors throw down their weapons; they might not have obeyed their chief's commands, if the fear of shame had not always been a ruling motive among Indians. In appealing to that Augustine had touched the right chord; the fear of contempt and of the accusation of ingratitude succeeded, when no eloquence would have done so.

Augustine hastened to pursue his advantage : he quickly freed Wenonda, and then turning to the Indians, said, " The Pequods are brave and true. The Good Spirit who lives above the clouds is pleased with His children, and will praise them. Red and white men will say alike, that the Pequods are great. They are as grateful as they are brave. Friends can trust them. They wished to avenge their white friend because they loved him. But when he begged for their prisoner's life they gave it to him, because he was their friend. The Pequods are a great people; none excel them in truth and courage. Their white friend will always be ready to come to them when they are ill."

Augustine's promise and his words of praise delighted the Indians, and turned their anger into joy. They danced about like happy children, and the woods rung with their shouts. Wenonda remained still, with his head down. Augustine turned to him with a smile, and said, "Will not the Fierce Wolf hasten through the woods, and return to his father? Uncas will receive him with joy."

Wenonda slowly raised his head, and looked at Augustine with unspeakable gratitude. Then he turned to the assembled Indians, and signed that he wished to speak to them. "Wenonda must speak," said the Fierce Wolf. "Wenonda must confess to the Pequods that he has done wrong. He hated the white man, though the white man loved him. Wenonda knows that now: he did not believe it before, though the white man saved him from death. The white man came to the Delawares' hunting-ground, and killed the stag Wenonda was pursuing. Wenonda was angry. The white man came to the Delawares' wigwams and asked for land, and the chief gave it. Wenonda could not help it, but his anger was great. He said to himself, 'The white man shall die. He has come over the salt water to rob the red men, to shoot their game, and to drive them from their homes.' Wenonda knew white men's ways. He had been in their huts, and knew their ways, and their greediness, their lies, and their cunning. Wenonda thought this white man and his friend were like the rest. He feared for his people, therefore he sought their life. Wenonda would have killed the white man, though he had saved him from the panther's claws. The Fierce Wolf howled with rage, for he thought the white men had come over the salt water to destroy his tribe. Then the bad spirit seized Uncas, and the white man cured him. Wenonda and the other warriors fell sick, and the medicine man cured them also. Wenonda wondered, and said to himself, 'This white man is not like his brothers.' Then the Pequods sent for him, and the white man went to them. Wenonda thought, 'It is well; if he is bad the Pequods will chase him from their huts, and Wenonda will not be called ungrateful.' Yet, when I was angry, I struck the white man's friend, and drove him from the village. Then the Pequods' message came, and Wenonda was to be given up. Wenonda thought he should die, till the white man came and freed him."

Wenonda was silent for a moment, and then turned to Augustine. "My brother, your love is more lasting than my hatred; you have conquered. Wenonda begs for your friendship. Will the white man forgive the Fierce Wolf?"

"I love you as a brother," Augustine cried; "hereafter, Augustine and Wenonda will be the truest of friends."

Then Wenonda spoke again. "Wenonda and the white man are brothers. Let us return to the Delawares; then the white man shall go over the salt water and bring his mother to our land. Wenonda will take care no harm comes to them. Wenonda owes his life to the white man: he will not forget his debt."

A shout from the Pequods showed Wenonda's words had pleased them; for, unforgiving as the Indians are for injuries, they are equally grateful for benefits. Though Augustine did not join in the shout, his heart was supremely happy. He had succeeded at last in his aim, and subdued his enemy by kindness; and no small joy was it, also, to think he might now bring his mother to America without fear.

While he was thanking God in his heart for these blessings, Natty seized his hand. "Truly," he said, "you have worked a miracle; I could not have believed such a thing was possible."

"Do not praise me," replied Augustine; "praise Him whose name is love, and who has commanded us to put away all anger and strife from our hearts."

"You were right," said Natty, greatly touched, "when you said love could work wonders; for Wenonda's present conduct is nothing short of a miracle."

The day was not too far advanced to prevent them reaching the Delaware village before nightfall. Augustine was anxious to start at once; and the Pequods did not oppose his wishes, unwilling as they were to part with him, when he represented to them what joy it would be to Uncas to see Wenonda again. The Pequod warriors accompanied them part of the way, and then left them with many assurances of future friendship, which were never broken.

It was late in the evening when Augustine, Natty, and Wenonda arrived at the Delaware village. Great, indeed, was the father's joy, when he saw the son whom he believed to be dead. Wenonda related what had happened, and nothing could then exceed the gratitude of the Indians. Flittah, especially, was wild with delight—Augustine himself was hardly more happy than she was that her brother was safe, and that he and Augustine were friends.

CHAPTER IX.

Now that all his difficulties were thus happily removed, Augustine had but few preparations to make before returning to Germany. His first care was to provide a house for his mother and sisters; but Natty, who saw his longing to depart at once, said, "Do not stay for that, Augustine: I promise you I will do all that is needful in your absence. If you will leave it all to me, I will answer for a hut being built, seed sown, and a piece of ground cleared—in short, all that is necessary shall be done; so start for Germany at once."

Augustine was only too happy to follow Natty's advice; so, after pointing out the place where he should wish the hut to be placed, he took leave of Natty and of the Delawares, to whom he repeated his promise of returning shortly. On his arrival at New

York, he found a ship just about to sail, in which he had a prosperous voyage to Bremen, when he hastened to visit Herr Strootsof, who listened to his adventures with the greatest interest, and heartily congratulated him upon his success.

Much to Augustine's regret, Captain Steding happened to be absent on a voyage to Copenhagen; but Herr Strootsof told him he would return shortly, and he promised he should remain in Bremen till Augustine's return.

"For," he said, "our old friend Steding himself shall take you all to New York in the finest ship I possess, and of course you shall all have a free passage." Augustine did not know how to be sufficiently grateful for his kindness.

"Now to business," interrupted Herr Strootsof. "There are many things you will want at your new settlement, which you can get here far better than at New York."

"I have thought about that," Augustine

replied, "and intended to ask your advice in the matter."

"Then leave it all to me," he returned. "When you come back to Bremen, you shall find all ready for you: I understand such affairs." Augustine again thanked him gratefully, and then hastened to his native town.

His heart beat fast as he came in sight of it. He quickened his pace, and was soon standing before the door of his home. He entered, and saw his mother and sisters. We must pass over their joyful meeting, and his recital of his adventures. Augustine told them of the beautiful land that was to be their future home, and eagerly were all preparations made for their voyage thither. Augustine carefully put all his own and his mother's affairs in order, before leaving his Fatherland for ever. Though he made all possible haste to do so, it was some weeks before all could be settled. At length they were able to start, and arrived safely in

Bremen, where they were all received at Herr Strootsof's house with the greatest kindness and courtesy. Joyfully did Augustine and Captain Steding meet again, as his host had promised they should do. Shortly before they were about to sail, Herr Strootsof took Augustine aside, and said to him, "Augustine, will you grant land to six or seven families who wish to emigrate? They would either pay you a small rent in return, or give you their services, as you may think best." Augustine was overjoyed at the proposal, for nothing could be more welcome to him than to have his fellow-countrymen for neighbours.

"They will be welcome, indeed," he replied. "My lands are large; there will be plenty of room for all."

"I thought you would be pleased," said Herr Strootsof, with a smile. "Here is the contract, ready drawn up for you to sign; the people are already on board my ship, for I have ventured to make an agreement in your name."

Augustine hastened to tell his mother the joyful news, which greatly softened to her the pain of leaving her native country. Herr Strootsof then gave Augustine a list of the things he had bought for him, which Augustine would have liked to have paid for at once. But this his host would not hear of, telling him instead that he was to settle everything with Captain Steding when they arrived at New York. There was nothing now left to be done but to take leave of kind Herr Strootsof and his wife, and to embark.

Their voyage was a prosperous one. As soon as they arrived at New York, Augustine wished to settle with Captain Steding about payment for his goods; but, to his astonishment, he learned from him that the grateful Strootsof had made him a present of the whole. Deeply touched with this great and most unexpected kindness, he charged Captain Steding with a grateful letter of acknowledgment, which the old captain promised to deliver. The next thing to be done was to purchase sumpter horses, for his mother and sisters' use for the journey inland, and also to carry their baggage. This done, they all took leave of Captain Steding, who said, as he parted with him, "Remember, I shall find you out some day, and spend my old age with you: keep a seat by your fireside for the old sailor." Augustine joyfully promised, and then the whole party started on their journey.

Nearly a year had passed since Augustine had left the Delaware village. It was now again a glorious summer's day when he reached his destination. But what a change had come over the place since then. He could hardly believe his eyes when he looked around. A considerable part of the wood had been cleared away, and rich corn was growing in its place. A large mansion was now standing on the little hill which overlooked the lake.

"What fairy can have done all this?" Augustine exclaimed. "Natty cannot have done all this with his own hands."

"Certainly not," answered Natty, as he rushed out of the house to greet the party. "This is the work of Uncas, and Wenonda, and Mahtoree, assisted by their grateful warriors. They have all been working for you when you were far away, and pleased, indeed, will they be if you will praise their work."

"Those good Indians!" exclaimed Augustine, deeply touched; "I will thank them at once."

Great was the joy of both Pequods and Delawares when they saw Augustine again, and received his grateful thanks. His mother and sisters were heartily welcomed to their new home; and soon he heard that it was Wenonda who had worked most indefatigably in his absence.

Another year passed happily away, and all continued to prosper. Captain Steding carried out his intention of joining the settlers, and was received by all with the greatest joy. Augustine (thus did the old man conclude his tale) lived long and happily. He was beloved by all the neighbouring Indians; but by none so much as by Wenonda, whose hatred he had so completely subdued. The settlement continued to flourish, as your own eyes can tell you. Let us all then cherish the name of Augustine; to whose goodness we owe all our present blessings. Let us remember that to live virtuously and industriously—to love God and our neighbours, is sure to lead to happiness in the end, no matter how many troubles may for a time come upon us; and if, in spite of all we can do, we find that we have enemies, let us think of the way in which Augustine softened the heart hard as iron with the coals of the fire of love.

LONDON:
Printed by Truscott, Son, & Simmons,
Suffolk Lane, City.

PUBLICATIONS
OF THE
Society for Promoting Christian Knowledge.

Most of these Works may be had in ornamental bindings, with gilt edges, at a small extra charge.

	Price.	
	s.	d.
A FEW MONTHS IN BORNEO. 18mo, cloth boards	1	0
A TALE OF TWO BROTHERS. By James F. Cobb, Esq. 18mo, cloth boards	1	6
ALONE AMONG THE ZULUS. By a Plain Woman. The Narrative of a Journey through the Zulu Country, South Africa. Fcap. 8vo, bevelled boards, gilt edges	2	6
ARCHIE GREY; or, Doing it Heartily. By the Author of "Harry's Battles," &c. 18mo, cloth boards	1	0
BATTLE WORTH FIGHTING, The, and other Stories. Fcap. 8vo, cloth boards	2	0
CARPENTER'S FAMILY, The: a Sketch of Village Life. By Mrs. Joseph Lamb (Ruth Buck). With four full-page Engravings on toned paper. Crown 8vo, cloth boards	2	0
CHARLEY WATSON, the Drunkard's little Son	1	6
CHURCH OF THE PATRIARCHS. Fcap. 8vo, limp cloth	1	0
CONFIRMATION CLASS, The; or, The History of a Year in Three Lives. By a Clergyman's Wife. Addressed to Village Girls. 18mo, cloth boards	1	6
CROYLAND ABBEY: an Historical Sketch. By the Rev. George G. Perry, Author of "History of the Crusades," &c. Fcap. 8vo, cloth boards	1	6
DIFFICULTY HILL, AND SOME LADS WHO CLIMBED IT. 18mo, cloth boards	1	6

PUBLICATIONS OF THE SOCIETY

	Price.
	s. d.
EARTH'S MANY VOICES. First and Second Series. With Illustrations on toned paper. Royal 16mo, extra cloth, gilt edges . . . . each	2 0
The two Series in one Volume	4 0
FETCHING AND KEEPING. 18mo, cloth boards . .	1 0
GOLD-STONE BROOCH, The. 18mo, cloth boards .	1 0
GRANNIE'S WARDROBE; or, The Lost Key. 18mo, cloth boards	1 0
GRETCHEN'S TROUBLES. 18mo, cloth boards . .	1 0
HERBERT GRAHAM. 18mo, cloth boards . . .	1 0
HISTORY OF FRANCE. From the Earliest Times to the Second Empire. 2 Vols. Fcap. 8vo, cloth boards	12 0
HOME IN SOUTH AFRICA. By the Author of "Alone among the Zulus." Fcap. 8vo, cloth boards . .	1 6
HOW TO MAKE A STEAM ENGINE. Fcap. 8vo, limp cloth	2 6
HUGH WYNFORD; or, The Cousin's Revenge. Fcap. 8vo, cloth boards	2 0
"IT ISN'T RIGHT;" or, Frank Johnson's Reason. By Mrs. Joseph Lamb (Ruth Buck) . . .	1 6
JOY OF WELL-DOING, The. 18mo, cloth boards .	1 0
LIKE AND UNLIKE. 18mo, cloth boards . .	1 6
LINDA. By the Author of "Maude Grenville." Crown 8vo, cloth boards	1 6
LIONEL'S REVENGE; or, The Young Royalists. Fcap. 8vo, cloth boards	2 6
MARGARET LESLIE. Fcap. 8vo, cloth boards . .	2 6
MARTIN HILL'S CHARGE. 18mo, cloth boards . .	1 0
MINTY, the Policeman's Foundling. 18mo, cloth boards	1 6
MOTHERLESS LADS, The; or, George West and his Brother Tom. 18mo, cloth boards . . .	1 6
NATURAL HISTORY OF THE BIBLE, The. By the Rev. H. B. Tristram, M.A., F.L.S. . . .	7 6

FOR PROMOTING CHRISTIAN KNOWLEDGE.

	Price.
	s. d.
NATURAL HISTORY OF BIRDS, The: a popular Introduction to Ornithology. By T. Rymer Jones, Esq., F.R.S. Illustrated with nearly 300 Engravings	9 0
OLIVE, THE TEACHER. 18mo, cloth boards	1 6
PHILIP MAVOR; or, Life among the Kaffirs. By W. H. G. Kingston, Esq. 18mo, cloth boards	1 0
PHILLIS; or, The Jealous One. 18mo, cloth boards	1 6
PICTURES AND STORIES FOR LITTLE CHILDREN. By Isabella E. Glennie. 18mo, cloth boards	1 0
PITCAIRN; with a short Notice of the Original Settlement and present Condition of Norfolk Island. By the late Rev. T. B. Murray, M.A. Fcap. 8vo, cloth boards	2 0
POOR LITTLE GASPARD'S DRUM: a Tale of the French Revolution. Fcap. 8vo, cloth boards	1 6
RECOLLECTIONS OF A VISIT TO BRITISH KAFFRARIA. Fcap. 8vo, cloth boards	2 0
ROB NIXON, THE OLD WHITE TRAPPER. By W. H. G. Kingston, Esq. 18mo, cloth boards	1 6
SANDWICH ISLANDS AND THEIR PEOPLE, The. By M. A. Donne, Author of "Denmark and its People," &c. Fcap. 8vo, cloth boards	2 0
SHORT STORIES FOUNDED ON EUROPEAN HISTORY: FRANCE, ITALY, SPAIN, SWEDEN, SWITZERLAND. 16mo . . . . each	2 0
STORIES FOR EVERY SUNDAY IN THE CHRISTIAN YEAR. Fcap. 8vo, cloth boards	2 0
STORIES ON "MY DUTY TOWARDS GOD." Crown 8vo, cloth boards	1 6
STORIES ON "MY DUTY TOWARDS MY NEIGHBOUR." Crown 8vo, cloth boards	2 0
TALES AND ALLEGORIES. On Toned Paper, Demy 16mo, gilt edges	1 0
TOM BARTON'S TRIAL, and other Stories. 18mo, cloth boards	1 0

PUBLICATIONS OF THE SOCIETY.

	Price.
	s. d.
TOM NEAL AND SARAH HIS WIFE, THE EXPERIENCES OF. Crown 8vo, cloth boards	1 6
TOY BOOKS FOR CHILDREN. In an Ornamental Cover. Demy 4to, each containing six large colored plates, with descriptive Letterpress in large type :—	
I.—PRETTY PICTURES OF PRETTY BIRDS	1 0
II.—BUTTERCUPS AND DAISIES, AND OTHER PRETTY FLOWERS	1 0
TRAVELS IN NORWAY. For Children. By Uncle John	1 0
URSULA'S GIRLHOOD. Fcap. 8vo, cloth boards	1 6
VICTOR LECZINSKI; or, The Road to Siberia. 18mo, cloth boards	1 0
WINIFRED LEIGH. By the Author of "Harry's Battles," &c. Fcap. 8vo, cloth boards	1 6
WINNIE'S DIFFICULTIES; or, "Which are my Duties?" Fcap. 8vo, cloth boards	1 6
WOODBURY FARM. 18mo, cloth boards	1 6
WRECK OF THE OSPREY, The: a Story for Boys. Fcap. 8vo, cloth boards	1 6

NEW COTTAGE WALL PRINTS,
PRINTED IN COLORS,
From Original Drawings by Eminent Artists.

Size, 14 by 11 inches.

HAYFIELD.	TRAWLING BY NIGHT.
CORNFIELD.	STORM.
STRAWYARD.	BIRD'S NEST.

Each 6d., in glazed frames 1s., in gilt frames 2s.

Depositories:
77, GREAT QUEEN STREET, LINCOLN'S INN FIELDS;
4, ROYAL EXCHANGE; 48, PICCADILLY;
AND BY ALL BOOKSELLERS.

PUBLICATIONS
OF THE
Society for Promoting Christian Knowledge.

Most of these Works may be had in ornamental bindings, with gilt edges, at a small extra charge.

	Price.
	s. d.
A TALE OF TWO BROTHERS. By James F. Cobb, Esq. 18mo., cloth boards	1 6
ALONE AMONG THE ZULUS. By a Plain Woman. The Narrative of a Journey through the Zulu Country, South Africa. Fcap. 8vo., bevelled boards, gilt edges	2 6
ANIMAL CREATION, The; a popular introduction to Zoology. By Thomas Rymer Jones, Esq., Professor of Natural History and Comparative Anatomy in King's College, London. Illustrated with nearly 500 engravings, 12mo., cloth boards	7 6
ASTRONOMY WITHOUT MATHEMATICS. By E. B. Denison, Esq., LL.D., Q.C. Fcap. 8vo., cloth boards. New edition, revised and enlarged	3 0
AUSTRALIA; its Physical Features, Inhabitants, Natural History, and Productions, &c., &c., together with an account of its various British Colonies; with map and six full page illustrations. Fcap. 8vo.	3 6
BATTLE WORTH FIGHTING, and other STORIES. Fcap. 8vo., cloth boards	2 0

	Price.	
	s.	d.

BIBLE PICTURE BOOK, complete, containing 96 plates, printed in three colors. Cloth boards . . 5 0
  In two vols.:—OLD AND NEW TESTAMENT. Limp cloth . . . . each 2 0
BIBLE PICTURES AND STORIES. In two vols. With 96 plates, printed in colors:—OLD AND NEW TESTAMENT. Extra cloth gilt . . each 7 0
BRITISH BIRDS IN THEIR HAUNTS. By the Rev. C. A. Johns 12 0
CARPENTER'S FAMILY, The; a Sketch of Village Life. By Mrs. Joseph Lamb (Ruth Buck). With four full page engravings on toned paper. Crown 8vo., cloth boards 2 0
CHARLEY WATSON, the Drunkard's little Son . . 1 6
CHEMISTRY OF CREATION; a Sketch of the Chief Chemical and Physical Phenomena of the Earth, Air, and Ocean. By Robert Ellis, F.L S., &c. &c., Fcap. 8vo., cloth boards. New and revised edition 5 0
COLONIAL EMPIRE of GREAT BRITAIN, The; considered chiefly with reference to its Physical Geography and Industrial Productions. In four vols, Fcap. 8vo., cloth boards. Vol. I. . . 1 6
  Vol. II. to IV., each 2 0
CONFIRMATION CLASS, The; or, the History of a Year in Three Lives. By a Clergyman's Wife. Addressed to Village Girls. 18mo., cloth boards . 1 6
DEWDROP AND THE MIST. By Charles Tomlinson, Esq. New Edition 3 6
DIFFICULTY HILL, and SOME LADS WHO CLIMBED IT. 18mo., cloth boards 1 6
EARTH'S MANY VOICES. First and Second Series. With Illustrations, on toned paper. Royal 16mo., extra cloth, gilt edges, each 2 0
  The two series in one volume 4 0

	Price.	
	s.	d.
EDNA WILLIS; or, the Promise Fulfilled. 18mo., cloth boards	1	0
ELDAD THE PILGRIM; a Sketch of the Manners and Customs of the Jews in the Century preceding the Advent of Our Saviour. Fcap. 8vo., cloth boards	3	0
EVENINGS at the MICROSCOPE; or Researches among the Minuter Organs and Forms of Animal Life. By P. H. Gosse, F.R.S. Post 8vo., cloth boards	6	0
FATHER AND DAUGHTER. 18mo., cloth boards	1	0
FETCHING AND KEEPING. Ditto ditto	1	0
FLOWERING PLANTS, GRASSES, AND FERNS OF GREAT BRITAIN. By Anne Pratt. New Edition. In four volumes, containing 319 colored plates. Gilt edges	42	0
FLOWERS of the FIELD. By Rev. C. A. Johns. Sixth edition. Fcap. 8vo., cloth boards	7	0
FOREST TREES. Two vols. By ditto ditto	7	6
FOREST TREES of BRITAIN. By Rev. C. A. Johns. Fcap. 8vo., cloth boards	7	0
FOUR SEASONS, The. Containing 40 plates, printed in colors, with descriptive Poetry. Royal 16mo., gilt edges	5	0
GEORGE COX'S REPENTANCE. 18mo., cloth boards	2	0
GOLD-STONE BROOCH, The. Ditto ditto	1	0
HEARTHSTONE BOY, The. 18mo., cloth boards	1	6
HISTORY of the CRUSADES, with four full page engravings. By G. G. Perry, M.A. Fcap. 8vo., cloth boards, gilt edges	2	6
HOW WE DINE; or, "Dinner's Ready." 18mo., cloth boards	1	6

	Price	
	s.	d.
HUGH WYNFORD; or, the Cousin's Revenge. Fcap. 8vo., cloth boards	2	0
HYMNS AND PICTURES. 16 colored plates, 4to., bevelled boards, gilt edges	4	0
———————— Second series, do. do.	4	0
The two series in one volume	8	0
"IT ISN'T RIGHT;" or Frank Johnson's Reason. By Mrs. Joseph Lamb (Ruth Buck)	1	6
LAND OF ISRAEL, The: A Journey of Travels in Palestine, undertaken with special reference to its Physical Character. By H. B. Tristram, M.A., F.L.S. Second edition. 8vo., cloth boards, with maps and colored plates	21	0
LIKE AND UNLIKE. 18mo., cloth boards	1	6
LINDA. By the Author of "Maude Grenville." Crown 8vo., cloth boards	1	6
LIVES of MISSIONARIES. Fcap. 8vo., cloth boards:—		
GREENLAND	2	0
SOUTHERN INDIA	3	0
NORTH AMERICA	2	6
INDIA, two vols., each	3	0
MARGARET LESLIE. Fcap. 8vo., cloth boards	2	6
MAURITIUS; being an Account of the Island, its History, Geography, Products, and Inhabitants. By Rev. F. P. Flemyng, M.A., F.R.G.S. With a Map and numerous Illustrations. Fcap. 8vo., cloth boards	2	6
MINTY, the Policeman's Foundling. 18mo., cloth boards	1	6
MOTHERLESS LADS, The; or, George West and his Brother Tom. 18mo., cloth boards	1	6

	Price	
	s.	d.
NATURAL HISTORY, Illustrated Sketches of. First and second series. Fcap. 8vo., cloth boards, each	2	6
NATURAL HISTORY PRINTS, with Letterpress Descriptions, containing 210 pictures. Half morocco, cloth sides, gilt edges . . . . plain	42	0
———————————————————————colored	63	0
OCEAN, The. By P. H. Gosse, F.R.S. Post 8vo., cloth boards	4	6
OLIVE, THE TEACHER. 18mo., cloth boards . .	1	6
OUR NATIVE SONGSTERS. By Anne Pratt. 73 colored plates. Royal 16mo., cloth boards . . .	8	0
PENNY WISE AND POUND FOOLISH. By Mrs. Carey Brock. Fcap. 8vo., cloth boards . . .	2	6
PEOPLE OF EUROPE. First and second series in a vol. 24 colored plates. Royal 16mo., limp cloth . .	2	6
PERSEVERANCE UNDER DIFFICULTIES, as shown in the Lives of Great Men. Fcap. 8vo., cloth boards	2	6
PHILIP MAVOR; or, Life among the Kaffirs. By W. H. G. Kingston, Esq. 18mo., cloth boards . .	1	0
PHILLIS; or, the Jealous One	1	6
PICTURES AND STORIES FOR LITTLE CHILDREN. By Isabella E. Glennie. 18mo., cloth boards . .	1	0
PITCAIRN; with a short Notice of the Original Settlement and present Condition of Norfolk Island. By the late Rev. T. B. Murray, M.A. Fcap. 8vo., cloth boards	2	0
RECOLLECTIONS OF A VISIT TO BRITISH KAFFRARIA. Fcap. 8vo., cloth boards	2	0
ROBINSON CRUSOE. New Edition. With 4 page engravings. 12mo., cloth boards . . .	3	0
ROB NIXON, THE OLD WHITE TRAPPER. By W. H. G. Kingston, Esq. 18mo., cloth boards .	1	6

	Price.
	s. d.

ROME AND ITS RUINS, with a Map and eight full page engravings. By W. Forsyth, Esq., Q.C. Fcap. 8vo., cloth boards, gilt edges 2 6

SANDWICH ISLANDS AND THEIR PEOPLE, The. By M. A. Donne, Author of "Denmark and its People," &c. Fcap. 8vo., cloth boards . . . 2 0

SCRIPTURE MANNERS and CUSTOMS. Fcap. 8vo., cloth boards 6 0

SCRIPTURE TOPOGRAPHY. PALESTINE. With Maps. Fcap. 8vo., cloth boards 6 0

SCRIPTURE TOPOGRAPHY. GENTILE WORLD. With Map. Fcap. 8vo., cloth boards . . . 6 0

SCRIPTURE NATURAL HISTORY. Fcap. 8vo., cloth boards 6 0

SELBORNE, NATURAL HISTORY OF. By the late Rev. Gilbert White, A.M. Arranged for Young Persons. A new and revised Edition Post 8vo., cloth boards 5 0

SHIPWRECKS and ADVENTURES at SEA. Fcap. 8vo., cloth boards 2 6

SHORT STORIES FOUNDED ON EUROPEAN HISTORY.— FRANCE, ITALY, SPAIN, SWEDEN, SWITZERLAND, 16mo., each 2 0

SKETCHES of the AFRICAN KINGDOMS and PEOPLES; with a map and numerous illustrations. Fcap. 8vo., cloth boards 4 0

STORIES FOR EVERY SUNDAY IN THE CHRISTIAN YEAR. Fcap. 8vo., cloth boards 2 0

———— on "MY DUTY TOWARDS GOD." Crown 8vo., cloth boards 1 6

———— on "MY DUTY TOWARDS MY NEIGHBOUR." Crown 8vo., cloth boards 2 0

	Price
	s. d.

TOM BARTON'S TRIAL, and other Stories. 18mo., cloth boards 1 0

TOM NEAL AND SARAH HIS WIFE, The EXPERIENCES OF. Crown 8vo., cloth boards 1 6

TOY BOOKS FOR CHILDREN. In an Ornamental Cover. Demy 4to., each containing six large colored plates, with descriptive Letterpress in large type :—

    I.—PRETTY PICTURES OF PRETTY BIRDS . 1 0

    II.—BUTTERCUPS AND DAISIES AND OTHER PRETTY FLOWERS 1 0

TRAVELS BY LAND AND SEA; The Old Arm Chair. Fcap. 8vo., cloth boards 3 0

VICTOR: a Tale of the Great Persecution. Fcap. 8vo., cloth boards, gilt edges 1 6

VICTOR LECZINSKI; or, the Road to Siberia. 18mo., cloth boards 1 0

WILD FLOWERS. By Ann Pratt. In two vols., containing 192 plates, printed in colors. 16mo., cloth boards 16 0

WINIFRED LEIGH. By the Author of "Harry's Battles," &c. Fcap. 8vo., cloth boards . . 1 6

WINNIE'S DIFFICULTIES; or, "Which are my Duties?" Fcap. 8vo., cloth boards 1 6

WOODBURY FARM. 18mo., cloth boards . . . 1 6

WRECK OF THE OSPREY, The; a Story for Boys. Fcap. 8vo., cloth boards 1 6

YEAR OF COUNTRY LIFE; or, Chronicle of the Young Naturalists. Fcap. 8vo., cloth boards . . 2 6

NEW COTTAGE WALL PRINTS.

PRINTED IN COLORS,

From Original Drawings by Eminent Artists.

Size 14 by 11 inches.

HAYFIELD,	TRAWLING BY NIGHT,
CORNFIELD,	STORM,
STRAWYARD,	BIRD'S NEST.

Each 6*d*., in glazed frames 1*s*., in gilt frames 2*s*.

Depositories:

77, GREAT QUEEN STREET, LINCOLN'S INN FIELDS;
4, ROYAL EXCHANGE; 48, PICCADILLY
AND BY ALL BOOKSELLERS.

Check Out More Titles From HardPress Classics Series In this collection we are offering thousands of classic and hard to find books. This series spans a vast array of subjects – so you are bound to find something of interest to enjoy reading and learning about.

Subjects:
Architecture
Art
Biography & Autobiography
Body, Mind &Spirit
Children & Young Adult
Dramas
Education
Fiction
History
Language Arts & Disciplines
Law
Literary Collections
Music
Poetry
Psychology
Science
…and many more.

Visit us at www.hardpress.net

personalised classic books

"Beautiful gift, lovely finish.
My Niece loves it, so precious!"

Helen R Brumfieldon

★★★★★

FOR KIDS, PARTNERS
AND FRIENDS

Timeless books such as:

Alice in Wonderland • The Jungle Book • The Wonderful Wizard of Oz
Peter and Wendy • Robin Hood • The Prince and The Pauper
The Railway Children • Treasure Island • A Christmas Carol

Romeo and Juliet • Dracula

| **Highly** Customizable | **Change** Books Title | **Replace** Characters Names with yours | **Upload** Photo at inside page | **Add** Inscriptions |

Visit
ImTheStory.com
and order yours today!

CPSIA information can be obtained
at www.ICGtesting.com
Printed in the USA
BVHW081020130819
555775BV00019B/1470/P